THE
YIN-YANG
JOURNAL

THE YIN-YANG JOURNAL

AN ALTERNATIVE READING OF THE TAO TE CHING

R C Allen

Inner Eye Press, Tucson, Arizona

Library of Congress Cataloging-in-Publication Data
Allen, Rupert C.
    The yin-yang journal : an alternative reading of the
Tao te ching / Rupert C. Allen.
        p. cm.
    Includes bibliographic references
    ISBN 1-880703-11-4
    1. Lao-tze. Tao te ching. 2. Philosophy, Taoist.   I. Title.
BL 1900.L35A86   1996
299'.51482–dc20

Cover design by Kimura/Bingham, Tucson, Arizona

Inner Eye Press
P. O. Box 5126
Tucson AZ 85703

For Linda

Contents

Why is it hard to rule Psyche?
It is because all within
know more than ego.

65

Five Easy Taoist Pieces

"Know male but keep to female "

This version of the *Tao Te Ching* is my extrapolation of Lao Tzu's premise that wise development of Psyche means downplaying ego's role. Ego is an illusion that must not be allowed to throw Psyche off balance. Ego is selfish—*egoísta,* as they say in Spanish—and soon becomes a tyrant. In a patriarchy this is especially true of men.

At one level Lao Tzu is addressing patriarchal men and announcing that the macho ego is the ruin of the Spirit: "Know the masculine, but keep to the feminine." (28)

Lao Tzu uses a telegraphic style, a kind of Basic Chinese. Collating a dozen or so English translations gives a sense of their common origin. Once we identify the Chinese character Lao Tzu has used, the question becomes, "How do we understand that concept, Chinese or no Chinese?" If Lao Tzu writes, "Know male, but keep to female," what does this mean in terms of Psyche?

Indeed, when Lao Tzu speaks of the "sage" or "wise man," what does he have in mind? The present version of the *Tao Te Ching* explores a fresh answer, for I believe that Lao Tzu had a vision of "wisdom" that the patriarchal scholar easily disregards: ego-transcendence in favor of the Creative Unconscious.

Translators of Lao Tzu are of two general classes—extravert and introvert, to borrow Jung's distinction. Both are valid according to the reader's temperament. Some see the *Tao Te Ching* as a book about interacting with society. I see it as a book about ego interacting with Psyche, i.e., *individuating*. I call this the evolution from yang-yin mind to yin-yang mind.

Yin and Yang

Yin and Yang are the dynamic duo of relativity, like the crest and the trough of a wave. They are not "opposites," for "opposite" is a static notion and suggests enmity, as in "the opposite sex."

For me the ocean wave is a good image for the life of Psyche. The crest is ego-consciousness, what I call yang. The trough is the Creative Unconscious, what I call yin. Yang-yin psyche is one where ego dominates. In yin-yang psyche the Creative Unconscious holds sway. Lao Tzu is telling the patriarchs that yang-yin mind should evolve into yin-yang mind. This is why Taoists always speak of "yin-yang," not "yang-yin."

Throughout the course of his inspired trip, Lao Tzu keeps coming up with new ideas about the contrast between yang-yin and yin-yang minds—how the latter fosters spiritual growth and how the former stifles it.

Psyche is a Walden Pond, teeming with a secret life. When in the summertime Thoreau lay still in his boat and floated on Walden Pond, a yin-yang Self emerged with great power, and the boat became a womb.

Psyche is alive with flora and fauna—what I call "all within." When we dream in our sleep, we experience Nature herself speaking to ego-consciousness, guiding it toward the Center.

The People, Yes!

The Chinese character *màhn* (see Choy, No. 1590), "people, citizens" is used often in the *Tao Te Ching*. In terms of the Individuation Process (evolution of the individual psyche) the "people" are what I call "all within." These "citizens" of the psyche are the numerous spiritual elements that make up the Country of Psyche, under the leadership of ego.

As a leader of "all within," ego can be a tyrant or a shepherd: a Mussolini or a Lincoln. "Bad" ego uses Psyche to its own advantage, whereas "good" ego, like an inspired artist, uses its position as a showcase for Psyche and does not take credit. All within are recognized.

But in the beginning ego is concerned with its own existence *apart* from Mother Nature. She is the "other," which allows ego to conceive of its own self. Ego, in order to exist at all, must experience itself as being beyond mere instinctual behavior. The other creatures are immersed in Instinct, whereas ego stands apart. The more ego succeeds in ego-consciousness, the more it views Instinct with suspicion. Hence yang-yin mind.

Our monotheism—the notion of a God separate from Nature (a cosmic Father)—reflects the male ego's view of itself as separate from the instinctual nature of Psyche. Male ego indeed makes God in its own image. Ego lords it over Psyche, and so images a God who lords it over the Earth.

The Chinese insight of yin-yang inspired the *Tao Te Ching*. Yin-yang allows yang-yin to grasp an alternative. One does not have to be anti-Nature and pro-God; yang-yin mind can grasp the idea of reversing the priority. Yang-yin can become yin-yang. This, to me, is the primary idea of the *Tao Te Ching*.

The Guru

I regard Lao Tzu as a guru, not as a teacher. For us Out West a "teacher" is an authority figure representing the system—a schoolmaster, the hotshot professor, the poet laureate. But in Asia a guru is an authoritative figure who embodies *individual* spiritual growth. The "authority" is actually charisma. A guru can be anyone who is living successfully at the spiritual level that you, as a virgin, have just glimpsed. Suddenly you recognize in that person a veteran of that spiritual level. Hence the saying, "When you are ready, the guru appears."

For a while you stay close to that person because of the new vibes that you are now absorbing, like fresh ocean air. This person has made a successful life based on the insight that was new to you. It is as if you were learning a new language and can suddenly recognize a native speaker. This is basically what a guru is.

Thus for me, Lao Tzu is a guru. I was ready for the yin-yang life and Lao Tzu appeared in the form of the *Tao Te Ching*. I had never doubted the rightness of yin-yang life, and all of his ideas were very nutritious food for thought.

When yin-yang people read the *Tao Te Ching,*
they latch onto it.
When yang-yin people read the *Tao Te Ching,*
they don't get it.
If such were not the case,
you wouldn't be able to recognize the Tao.

41

Reality and the *Tao Te Ching*

For many years I've been aware of people in social intercourse as actors playing roles. This includes myself. We do just what professional actors do on stage: we play roles, take on personae.

Persona come from L. *per-sonare*, "to sound through." This refers to the megaphone that actors in ancient times would use to project their voices into an amphitheater. The megaphone was a "sound-through," and *per-sonare* belongs to a group of word formations based on the idea of "sounding": *re-sonare*, to resound; *con-sonant*, "sounding with," and so forth.

Actors often become identified with a certain character or persona ("type-casting"). They may come to think that their screen presence is actually who they "really" are. I've read that this happened to John Wayne, as the Hero, the tough hombre who is the Good Guy in the melodrama of life. What we call a "great" actor seem to be one who creates each role so convincingly that we experience the character and not the actor playing the role.

How does all this apply to our daily reality? We play different roles every day (e.g., the professional persona and the domestic persona), but we are not accustomed to think that there might be an alternative reality. The ego-persona says, "What you see is what you get." It's hard to get past this brainwashing. It's hard to realize that an alternative reality exists.

But that's why poets exist. I believe—along with Jung and Lao Tzu—that the great task and joy of living your life consists of discovering an alternative reality to the social persona assigned to you, to *transcend* its limitations.

Jung called this transcendence the Individuation Process; Lao Tzu called it the Way, the Tao. The idea of yin-yang and yang-yin allowed him to grasp the fact that in each person Psyche could be oriented either way: in favor of yang or in favor of yin.

Yang-yin gives yang top billing; it is dominated by the social or patriarchal ego and uses the resources of Psyche for its own selfish advantage. In the yin-yang mind Psyche is the Creative Unconscious, and She is treated as the basic reality of life.

Lao Tzu, as a transcendentalist, clearly saw that human consciousness is a Way developed by Mother Nature in order to become conscious of Herself. This is the Tao.

In every generation there are always a few who realize that the social reality is a yang-yin proposition, meaning that the priority can be reversed. Once you get the idea of yin and yang, you begin to realize that yang-yin can be turned into yin-yang.

I first realized this when I read Henri Bergson's great book

I first realized this when I read Henri Bergson's great book *Creative Evolution.* It worked in my heart like a yeast. Bergson's dialectic wasn't yin/yang; it was Being/Becoming. Now I realize that yang-yin mind is static (Being), while yin-yang mind is dynamic (Becoming). Yin-yang mind *evolves creatively* (to paraphrase Bergson's title).

To yang-yin (ego-dominated) mind, "reality" is that which is named. To yin-yang mind (attuned to instinct), "reality" is that which has no name. Our best poets are people seeking to name that which has no name.

East and West differ on this basic point. To Asians, our "named reality" is maya, an illusion. It is merely "sounding through" the megaphone of ego. Maya is a movie we are attending. Ego is a Hollywood dream machine.

Tribal cultures favor yin-yang priority. They treat their society as a ritual whose underlying reality is Mother Earth, intuited as what we call Psyche. Human consciousness is one of Mother Nature's amazing feats, and to "individuate" means to let Her become conscious in your heart. As tribal people say, to be human is to think with your heart.

This, I believe, is the main message of the *Tao Te Ching:* think with your heart. In yang-yin mind ego functions as the "boss." Yin-yang mind follows the Tao of Nature, where there is no "boss"—yet everything gets done.

THE YIN-YANG JOURNAL

1

The paths men take are named.
My path, ever emergent,
cannot be named.
Nameless it is,
the beginning of night and day,
the Mother of myriad consciousness.

Non-ego mind lives a Mystery;
ego-mind names, and covets the names.
Both have the same Source:
though called differently,
both are mysteries in themselves.

To understand these words,
be conscious of the Mystery.
Abide in the Valley.

2

Her beauty teaches you non-beauty.
Compared with Her,
what people call "beautiful"
is not beautiful.
Indeed, mystery and non-mystery
give birth to each other.
People scorn mystery,
but mystery is the Gateway.

Opposites dramatize each other:
long/short, high/low, front/back. . .
People want "drama," not mystery.

So the wise ones keep a low profile.
They embrace, but do not possess.

Whatever happens is neither to our blame
nor to our credit.
Because we do not take credit,
nobody can take it away.

3

Without inflated egos
there are no quarrels.
Without treasured expectations
there is no burglary.

If you love Her wisely
you will forget ambition
and take dinner together.

Do not strive;
relax and enjoy.
Then all will be well.

4

She is receptive.
You see how receptiveness
cannot be "filled,"
cannot be changed
by your entry.

She blunts the razor's edge.
untangles the knot,
softens the glare,
subdues turmoil.

A deep pool She is,
the Source.
Where does all this come from?
It comes from Her,
our common Ancestress.

5

Natural Self is not sentimental.
She treats ego as a dummy.
Wise up and do likewise.

Mother Nature breathes in and out,
like lungs.
Each breath is a season of the year.
Don't worry about naming it;
just breathe.

6

The Valley persists.
She is the Mystery.
She is the Gateway to the Center.
Revere Her:
She is inexhaustible.

7

The Natural Self abides forever.
What is the secret?
She is beyond our clock time.
Wise up: there's no need to be
"up-to-date."
Dig the Natural Self.

8

Like water, She is the highest good.
She benefits by flowing, not striving.
She flows as men do not.
She is the Way.

Hug your planet.
Think with your heart.
Don't let others stress you out.
Speak truly.

Don't let ego dictate to Psyche.
Do your thing without beating around the bush.

Above all, be aware of your timing,
for timing is everything.

9

Do not be greedy.
Recognize what is there,
and be content.
Do not presume to oversharpen
the edge of desire.
This treasure cannot be counted,
like money,
nor can a bank protect it.
Relax
and go with the Inner Flow.

10

With body and soul
can you stay centered as yin-yang?

Can you relax
and breathe as in the Womb?

In cultivating the inner vision
can you transcend ego-static?

Loving all within
can you be artless?

In using the five senses
can you be receptive like Her?

Being open to all within (as in a dream)
can you resist yang-yin impulse?

Give birth and nurture,
without possessing.
Act, but take no credit.
Lead, but do not dominate.

This is Integrity.

11

Thirty spokes converge
at the center of the wheel.
It is the Center that matters,
not the number of spokes.

A clay pot prefigures
potential use of the space within.

Make doors and windows in your house:
this determines how you face the world.
The materials used make it possible
to transcend the materials.

12

Look beyond the colors that dazzle the eye.
Listen beyond the sounds that delight the ear.
Taste beyond the flavors that excite the palate.
Chasing after gratification for its own sake
throws the mind off center.

Gut-feeling is the best guide
when you relax and let Her lead.

13

Cultivate a modest ego.
Inflated ego is a misfortune to the Soul.
Ego asks,
"Why should I be modest?"
I say in answer:
when you treasure modesty
Soul has room to flourish.

Ego asks,
"How could I be a misfortune to the Soul?"
I say,
Because you are driven by selfishness.

Surrender humbly,
then we can trust you
to care for us.

Love Self more than you love "yourself"—
then we see you as steward of the Soul.

14

Look at me. Can you see me,
beyond form?
Listen to me. Can you hear me,
beyond sound?
Embrace me. Can you caress me,
beyond body?

I have no bright yang surface,
I have no dark yin depth.
No duality.
Seamless, unnameable,
I arise from a void
because ego makes me conscious.

Ego is one form; I am all forms.
Ego is one image; I am all images.
Ego defines; I am beyond defining.

Within,
there is no beginning, no end.
Abide with the ancient Way,
and be always in the Now.

Be aware of non-ego awareness;
this is the essence of yin-yang mind.

15

The tribal shamans are responsive to Nature.
Because of this ego cannot fathom them.
Ego can only describe their behavior.

They approach Her with respect,
like leaders testing an icy stream;
like cautious and courteous guests
they yield, all of a piece, like melting ice,
like an uncarved block of wood;
receptive, like a valley,
settling, like a muddied pool.

Can ego wait for the mud to settle?
Can ego relax and let things just happen?
Can ego travel the Way,
indifferent to its own fulfillment?

16

Empty the mind of all ego-matter.
Let the heart be at peace.
Before your very eyes
the seasons rise from the Source
and return.

Go with Her Flow and find peace;
struggle with it and bring confusion.
Being open to all within,
ego will be the true leader of all;
being open to all within
gives rise to ideal climate.

In Nature no one does anything,
yet everything gets done.
Co-exist with all within,
and travel the Way.

What ego calls "death"
is not part of the equation.

17

The best ego is one
of whose existence
Psyche is barely aware,
such as the shaman.

Next is the one who lives serenely:
this makes for serenity within.

Then comes the fearful ego,
and then the ego that causes madness.

If yang does not trust yin,
then yin cannot trust yang.

The wise ego does not make speeches
to Psyche.
When creative works are made,
all within say,
"We did it!"

18

When ego becomes domineering,
then "ethics" appear:
moral/immoral, good/bad.
When Psyche feels mixed up,
ego conjures filial piety:
"Ye shall love your Father!"

Ego conjures Patriotism.

19

When ego gives up its high opinion of itself,
all within rejoice.
Get off the morality trip,
and all within will be fine.

Why censor Psyche?
This is self-defeating.
Enough with the dialectics!
Transcend the so-called needs
of ego.
Relax.

20

Please: no more existentialism.
Please: no more patriarchal philosophers.
They are so many popes
plugging their version of Reality.

Out there in the world
people feast on burgers
and watch parades.

Yin-yang mind seeks nothing,
because it's already here.

Yang-yin mind,
being bright and clever,
sees yin-yang as dim and weak.

Yin-yang's got no home
in their world anymore.
This is because yin-yang
is nourished by the Great Mother.

21

Practice yin-yang mind, not yang-yin mind.
This is the issue.

Yin-yang mind is elusive and intangible,
yet we practice it when we dream.
When we dream, all is dim and dark—
except for the dream, the oneiric drama.

The dream is very real;
when we dream our faith is total.

To this day human beings continue to dream,
and to relive yin-yang mind.
How do we know the ways of Nature?
Because we dream.

22

Yield and you will be whole.
Bend and you will not break.
Empty the mind of ego ambitions
and you will be fulfilled.
Let yang-yin mind wither;
be reborn as yin-yang mind.

The more you give up,
the more is given to you.
Have little, and be rich;
have much, and lose the Way.

Yin-yang mind seeks the Center,
and has the respect of us all.
Yin-yang mind does not try to be a star,
and so it shines.
Yin-yang mind does not get a swelled head,
and loves to feel our gratitude!

Yin-yang mind does not take credit for Psyche,
and so is soothed by our recognition.
Yin-yang mind does not compete,
hence we ourselves do not compete.

When ego is yin-yang,
we find it magnetic!

23

Only simple and quiet words will ripen.
Oratory and hot air come and go.
Monsoon is but a season.

Yang-yin mind is monsoon,
much ado about nothing.
If Heaven-and-Earth cannot make
an eternal monsoon,
how can yang-yin mind possibly do it?

Yin-yang mind is centripetal.
Yang-yin mind is centrifugal,
always fleeing from the Center,
like a fugitive
running for his life.

Trust us,
and we will trust you.

24

Ego lives on tiptoe.
It can't just stand there.
Ego strides along,
unwilling to stroll.

When ego shows off,
we are not amused.
When ego becomes self-righteous,
we turn off.
Yang-yin cannot endure
in the Land of Tao.
In Tao these things are called
"unwanted food and extraneous growths."

We all hate this.
Yin-yang mind forgets about all that stuff.

25

First there was One,
then there were two:
Heaven and Earth.

She,
alone, changeless,
Self-sufficient,
She is the Mother of All.

Impossible to name this insight.
I just call it The Way,
The Great Valley.

She flows eternally,
and never leaves us.

She is the Great Valley.
Heaven is the Great Valley.
Earth is the Great Valley.
Yin-yang mind is just like that.

Yin-yang mind
follows the ways of Heaven and Earth,
the ways of Self-becoming.

26

Earth's gravity
gives birth to ego-awareness,
when you think about it.

The Stillness
gives birth to our spirit.

Therefore the wise ones,
as they travel through life,
do not lose sight of their baggage.
Though the world offers many a spectacle,
they remain calm.

Why should the steward of inner wealth
be seduced by the spectacles of our day?
Why lose one's roots?
Why lose the stewardship?

27

Yin-yang progress is like flying:
it leaves no tracks.

Yin-yang speech
is completely self-consistent.

Self-knowledge uses no abacus.
Protection of Self needs no padlock,
because Self cannot be violated
in the first place.
I am bound to be with Her,
and no one can undo these ties.

Thus, the steward is available to all within,
and does not repress them.
What is "enlightenment,"
if not yin-yang mind?

Good ego is bad ego's guru.
Bad ego is good ego's obverse.
If you do not honor the guru,
if you do not respect the obverse,
you err, no matter how cleverly.
This is a basic truth.

28

Recognize machismo for what it is,
and stick with Her.
Be a river to Psyche!
Flow with Her
and rediscover non-ego awareness.

Know yang,
but stick with yin,
and be the model of the perfect steward,
true to Psyche
beyond the calendar.

Accept the world out there,
and drink from the Fountain within,
the Source.

When the block of marble is carved
it takes on meaning.
When yin-yang mind is the sculptor,
the steward is fulfilled.
As they say,
"The great tailor does minimal cutting."

29

Do you think that you can take over
and improve Her?
I do not believe it can be done.

She is a Special Vessel,
not a tool for ego.
Acting upon Her spoils things;
grasping at Her loses it.

All things have their rhythm—
growing, waning,
fervent, serene,
afoot, abed.

Yin-yang mind ignores ego-orders.

30

You need to represent Psyche,
without exalting ego.

If you truly lead Psyche,
you will not take the credit,
nor boast of your ability,
like a general.
War means laying waste.

Yin-yang mind "achieves,"
because it has no "choice."
It does its thing,
and forces nothing.

The idea of force
comes from the idea of weakness.
That is not the Way to go.
It can't last.

31

All within reject the weapons of ego.
Therefore yin-yang mind avoids weapons.

Yin-yang mind prefers the left hand.
Yang-yin mind prefers the right hand.

Yin-yang mind would no doubt use force
if given no choice,
but harmony within is nearest to the heart,
and "winning" is a Pyrrhic victory.

Yang-yin mind thinks that winning
is everything.
This makes yin-yang mind impossible.

Celebrate the left hand,
mourn the right hand,
the butcher.

32

The Path is always unmarked.
Unseen, it cannot be conquered
(as men "conquer" mountains).

If ego can venture within,
the forest creatures will respond.
Heaven and Earth unite,
and gentle rain begins to fall.
When ego stops commanding,
all within harmonize.

Analyze simplicity if you wish,
but know when enough is enough.

Tao in the world
is a river to the sea.

33

To understand other egos
is to be wise in the ways of the world.

To understand your own ego
is to be wise in the ways of Psyche.

To overcome others requires ego-power;
to transcend ego-power
requires strong non-ego desire.

What is wealth?
It is contentment with modest means.
Practice yin-yang mind
and you will stay whole.

Yin-yang mind is your home,
and will not pass away.

34

The Great Valley River floods all,
right and left.
All within live there,
down by the Riverside.
Ego does nothing,
yet everything gets done.

She nourishes all,
but does not tyrannize.
She goes unnoticed.
How humble,
and yet how great!

Why is She great?
It is because She is not a prima donna.
She is the Prima Donna of Earth,
but She is no prima donna.

35

Cleave to the Great Image,
and all within will rally around.
In peace and contentment they will come.

People mostly want to be entertained;
they regard yin-yang mind as so much tofu—
bland and without flavor.

Well, you can't taste it,
but it sustains the healthy Soul.

36

If you want to breathe out,
you have to breathe in.
There is no point to airless lungs.
The first thing is to breathe.
Before you inhale
you must exhale.
You inhale when you are weak.
You exhale when you are strong.

Stay in the swim
and avoid ego-weapons.

37

On this Path
there is no ego-action,
yet everything gets done.
If ego accepts this,
all within will develop naturally.
If, in growing,
they develop ego-desire,
one will turn again to yin-yang mind.
Without ego-desire
all within are at peace,
and all flourish in the natural state.

38

Natural Self is not Self-conscious.
That is its naturalness.

Ego-self is self-conscious,
and so is not natural.
In yin-yang mind
Natural Self—inspiration—
initiates action.
Ego does not.
This is called *wu-wei,*
"do nothing."
Why be otherwise?

Yang-yin mind keeps busy,
but accomplishes little.
Substantial humanity is Self-serving,
not self-serving.
Yang-yin mind is self-serving,
not Self-serving.
Like a harsh school principal
it wants to coerce the obedience
of all within.

When yin-yang mind languishes,
then we get "morality."
After than we get dry ceremony.

Dry ceremony does not speak to the Soul,
and creates confusion.
Yin-yang mind does not presume to call the shots,
because that is not the point.

Yin-yang mind dwells on the reality of Psyche,
and not on the illusion of ego-importance.
Yin-yang looks to the inner, not the outer.

39

The archetypes let us experience Centered Being:
The sky is whole and clear.
The Earth is whole and firm.
The gods are whole and strong.
The Valley is whole and overflowing.
Nature is whole and vital.
Yin-yang mind is whole and sound.

All these have integrity.
Without integrity the sky would crack and fall.
Without integrity the Earth would split apart.
Without integrity the gods would wither away.
Without integrity the Valley would dry up.
Without integrity Nature would become extinct.
Without integrity yin-yang mind
would become yang-yin mind.

Therefore non-ego is noble.
Our foundations lie low, in the Earth.
Yin-yang recognizes
that it is an orphan, bereft.
Yin-yang mind recognizes its roots.
Yang-yin mind regards itself as the Jewel of Psyche.
Yin-yang mind is solid as a rock.

40

Tao flows into us,
soft,
like water.

Yin-yang arises because
it takes two to tango.
But the Dance
precedes the dancers.

41

When yin-yang people read the *Tao Te Ching,*
they latch onto it.
When yang-yin people read the *Tao Te Ching,*
they don't get it.
When hicks hear about the *Tao Te Ching,*
they just laugh.

If such were not the case,
you wouldn't be able to recognize the Tao.

Thus it is said:
The Bright Path looks dim,
Evolving looks like no progress,
Going forward looks like going backward,
Natural Self looks like suicide,
Clarity of Self looks like muddy waters,
Abundance looks like starvation,
Solid appears hollow.

Earth has no corners.
Yin-yang mind is in no hurry.

The ear cannot hear the Great Sound.
The eye cannot see the Great Form.
The Path is hidden and nameless,
and brings to fruition all within.

42

This is the Way things are:
the Dance creates yin-yang;
yin-yang creates a third,
and so plurality becomes manifold.
All that you create embrace yang,
resting in yin,
blending into harmony.

Yang-yin mind hates the bastard state,
and hates to be a wimp;
yet yin-yang mind has no problem with this.

You gain by transcending ego-values,
and you lose by empowering ego.

I agree with Lao Tzu:
ego lives and dies
by doing violence to all within.
That's what the man said,
and you better believe it!

43

Yoni, the cushiest place of all,
subdues lingam,
the hardest throb of all.

The Cave pervades the spelunker.
Hence I know the value of Receptive Embrace.

Without words it teaches;
without ego-effort it fulfills.

44

Fame or Self: which matters more?
Self or bank account: which is more precious?
Which is more painful to lose?
Ego-attachment is the bane of our existence,
like hoarding wealth.

Being centered, yin-yang mind
is immune to disappointment.
Yin-yang mind is not greedy,
so there's plenty of time
for everything.

45

People see yin-yang mind
as much ado about nothing;
and yet,
it never ceases to amaze.

People see it as empty,
and yet,
it is a cornucopia.

In the water a straight stick
appears bent.
To yang-yin mind
yin-yang is pointless,
its eloquence nonsense.

But inspiration warms the heart,
and serenity transcends conflict.

Nature is centered;
let us be likewise.

46

When Psyche enjoys yin-yang mind
all within are fertilized.
When Psyche endures yang-yin mind,
war breaks out.

Ego-desire is the worst offense,
and to be malcontent
is to invite disaster.

If you know when enough is enough,
you will always have enough.

47

Without going out of your door
you can know yang-yin world.
Without looking through a window
you can know yin-yang world.

Without traveling,
you can know;
and you can name the unseen,
and you can achieve
without ego-striving.

48

The working yang-yin scholar
builds knowledge day by day.
Retired yin-yang scholar
sloughs knowledge
day by day.

Ease up on that professional knowledge,
and go for non-ego knowledge.
Then, nobody is doing anything,
yet everything gets done.

Which do you want—
their business,
or your Empire?

If Empire,
don't interfere.

49

Yin-yang ego is not selfish,
and sees to the desires of all within.
I am open to all,
I do not pick and choose.

This is yin-yang way.
I keep faith with all within,
in their comings and goings.

Yin-yang ego is modest.
All within look up.
Yin-yang ego
is a loving parent.

50

Some of us worry about longevity,
others don't.
If you know how to dream,
you won't have nightmares.

Why is this?
It is because yin-yang dreamer
turns away
from yang-yin intrusion.

51

All things arise from yin-yang,
not yang-yin.
She nourishes them,
shapes them,
and so all things
live within the Tao
spontaneously,
not out of obedience.

She is our life.
She develops, nurtures,
shelters, comforts—
gives without thought;
guides without ego.

This is yin-yang mind.

52

The beginning of the mind
is Mother Nature.
Knowing the Mother within,
you may know the offspring within.
Knowing these,
you stay in touch with Her,
and you live in the Now.

Return to the basics
and transcend ego-fears.

Shut your mouth,
guard your senses,
and enrich your life.
Join the public debate,

get "busy"—
and you waste your life.

Seek clarity within;
seek strength by yielding.
Use your light to find the Light;
live Now.

53

Having an inkling of yin-yang mind,
I fear the path of yang-yin mind.
Yin-yang Way is simple and easy,
yet yang-yin mind loves to be sidetracked.

The center of yin-yang mind is swept clean;
the fields of yang-yin mind are weedy,
and the granaries are empty.
Yang-yin ego wears the finest clothes,
has the latest weapons,
gorges at gourmet restaurants,
lives high on the hog.

Such a crime!
Yin-yang mind it's not!

54

Yin-yang, firmly established,
cannot be uprooted by yang-yin.

Embrace her,
and T'ai chi cannot be sundered.
In the end, all respect this.

Cultivate yin-yang in the Self,
and it will be who you are.
Cultivate it in Psyche,
and it will grow freely.

Within is a village,
a city, a state, a nation.
Cultivate it and it becomes universal.

You, the individual, are the nucleus.
You may be a "village,"
a "city," a "state," or a "nation."

How do I know this?
Because of this very experience.

55

Yin-yang mind
is akin to pre-ego mind.
Wasps, scorpions, and snakes,
sensing no threat,
leave it be.
Raptors and predators do not pounce.
Its skeleton is not rigid,
its muscles not hardened—
but its grasp is secure.

Yin-yang mind has a virginal arousal.
Its energy does not wilt,
because it is centered.

Knowing centeredness,
one knows constancy.

Knowing constancy,
one knows the light.

Are you in a hurry?
That is a bad sign!
Do you huff and puff?
You are forcing the issue!

Growing old before your time
is not the way of Tao,
and you will soon wither away.

56

Intuition cannot be put into words;
words cannot substitute for intuition.

Sit quietly,
close the doors,
dim the lights,
and simplify.

Tone down the highlights,
and let the dust settle.

Such is yin-yang identity.
Ego cannot cozy up to this one,
cannot snub,
harm, honor, or disgrace it.

Yin-yang mind is beyond all that.

57

Govern Psyche according to Nature's norm.
Consider conflict to be abnormal;
lead Psyche without striving.
Win Her over by letting Her be.
How do I know this?

Well,
because the more rules you make,
the poorer Psyche becomes;
the more efficient your weapons,
the greater Her confusion.
The more clever you become,
the weirder She turns.
The more rules and regulations,
the greater the crime rate.

Therefore yin-yang mind says:
I let well enough alone,
and all within settle down.
I enjoy harmony,
and all within function aright.
I relax,
and all within prosper.
I impose no desires,
and all within live simply.

58

When ego governs little,
all within remain in touch with Her.
When ego governs too much,
all within seek subterfuge.

Wholesome Psyche needs modest ego.
Macho ego is a spiritual calamity.
Who knows when the one becomes the other?
Who can say what is "normal"?
"Normal" ego easily becomes weird;
yang-yin ego loses its way,
and all within fall into confusion.

Therefore yin-yang ego
is sharp—but does not cut;
is pointed—but does not injure;
is straight—but does not overreach;
is bright—but does not dazzle.

59

In governing Psyche and serving Consciousness
Restraint is best.
Frugal ego is akin to pre-ego,
for it follows Her,
just as before.

With a good store of the Life Force,
creative action is easy,
and one does not think of limits.
There are no limits.

Such an ego
is fit to lead Psyche.
When you embrace the Mother
you are deeply rooted
and firmly founded.
You live long,
and your vision endures.

60

To govern Psyche
takes a gourmet touch,
like cooking a delicate little fish.

If you govern as yin-yang,
your demons lose their power
(not they they are weak,
but they will not contaminate all within,
just as yin-yang ego does not contaminate
all within).

Once the demons and the ego
are defused,
the Life Force flows freely.

61

Psyche is a Lowland
toward which all rivers flow.
It is a convergence of all within.
She, the Female, quiescently
absorbs the Male.
She seduces yin-yang mind
by lying underneath.
Modest ego seduces Psyche.
The one seduces by lying low,
the other, by yielding.

Mother Psyche, without motive,
wishes to protect all within;
modest ego, without motive,
wants to serve all within.
Each gets what it wants.
It is fitting that She should be a Valley.

62

T ao is the secret Source of all within.
It is the treasure of yin-yang mind,
but also preserves yang-yin mind.

Oratory is fine for the marketplace,
and philanthropy is respectable.
Why discard orators and philanthropists?

At the President's inaugural,
though you might bring expensive gifts,
it is better to offer a poem.

Why do poets honor the Tao?
Not for purpose of gain,
but because they find what they seek,
and are not harshly judged.
All within love the Tao of yin-yang.

63

Act through non-ego,
effortlessly.
Taste the untasted.
Magnify the microcosm.
Enhance the inner hints.

Do not resent slights to ego.
Approach the "difficult"
as simple play.
Realize achievement bit by bit.

In Nature nobody does anything,
yet everything gets done,
bit by bit.
Yin-yang mind is not ambitious,
and so accomplishes much.

Yang-yin mind, making big plans,
is riding for a fall.
Yin-yang mind recognizes ego-difficulties,
and steers clear.

64

The balance of Nature is not planned.
Without plans,
nothing can go awry.

Brittle ego is easily shattered;
being frail, it is easily scattered.

Act now, having the luxury,
and forestall confusion.

Great oaks from little acorns grow.
Great buildings begin with a heap of earth.
Great journeys begin with the first step.
Exert ego—and spoil it.
Lose by grasping.

Yin-yang is not driven by ego,
and so does not spoil Psyche;
does not grasp,
and so does not lose Her.

People often fail by smelling success.
Keep your original equilibrium,
and you will not fail.

Yin-yang mind desires to be desireless.
Antiques hold no interest,
especially antique notions.

Yin-yang mind seduces all within,
and they cease their transgressions.
In birthing Self-fulfillment
Yin-yang is midwife, nothing more.

65

The tribal shamans do not teach the people;
they keep them in the dark.

Why is it hard to rule Psyche?
It is because all within
know more than ego.

When ego tries to outwit them,
Psyche is the loser.
Ego without ingenuity
is a blessing on the land.

To know both kinds of ego
is to know one's preference.
The tribal ego is deep and far-reaching.
It leads all within
back to Harmony.

66

Why is the Sea superior to rivers?
Because it lies below.
Being inferior, it is superior.

If ego wants to be superior to all within,
it must be inferior to them all.
If ego wants to lead,
it must follow them.
Wise ego stays harmlessly in front,
like a wise coach.

Because Coach does not compete,
he meets no team resistance.

67

People say they admire yin-yang mind,
useless though it be.
(Give the poet a Nobel Prize.)

Life holds three Treasures:
Motherly Love,
Wise use of resources,
and Transcending ego-identity.

Motherly Love is courage itself.
Frugal husbandry creates abundance.
Transcending stardom,
ego becomes the true leader of all within.

Motherly love resolves all battles
and defends forever.

When yin-yang leads all within,
Motherly Love is the Guide to Salvation.

68

A good warrior does not brag.
A good fighter is not angry.
A good winner does not gloat.
A good employer serves the clerks.

This is what we may call
the Power of non-action,
the ability to deal with all within—
what the tribal people think of
as being in harmony.

69

If Psyche suffers civil war,
be a private, not a general.
Prefer retreat to advance.

This could be called
"marching in place";
"rolling up your sleeves";
"letting them draft you";
"going through the motions."

The greatest calamity
is to underestimate yang-yin ego.
When you do this,
you risk the Treasure within.

In a civil war
the protesters are right.

70

These words are easy to write,
understand, and put into practice.
But yang-yin mind cannot fathom them,
much less put them into practice.

Words have their Source,
and spiritual events have their Ancestress.
Yang-yin mind does not know this,
for it does not suspect
the existence of yin-yang mind.

Yin-yang mind is not commonly known,
for it rarely surfaces.
It keeps a low profile
and nourishes the Spirit.

71

To realize that ego-knowledge is ignorance:
this is a noble insight.

To regard ego-ignorance as knowledge
is sick.

Do you want to be well?
Then get sick of your sickness.

Yin-yang mind is not ill,
being sick of ego-sickness;
precisely for that
it is healthy.

72

When all within fear no power,
then yin-yang power has arrived.
Do not disturb them in their living.
When you do not weary them,
they are not wearied of you.

Thus, yin-yang mind has Self-knowledge,
and is self-effacing.

Yin-yang mind loves the Self,
but does not exalt self.
It transcends the one,
and adopts the other.

73

Daredevil ego gets wrecked;
dareless ego lives on.
For Psyche
one is beneficial,
and one is harmful.
Who knows why?
Each of the two egos
has its own explanation.

This is the Way of noble consciousness:
it overcomes without contending;
it answers without speaking;
it comes without being called;
it lives at ease with Nature's ways.

Her net is everywhere.
Its meshes seem wide,
yet it catches all.

74

When all within live beyond clock time,
why threaten to set the clock?
Suppose that all within obey the clock;
if one disobeys,
shall I seize and kill the one
who dares to disobey the clock?

Punishment is carried out by the executioner.
To take over the executioner's job
is to imagine chopping wood
as a master carpenter might chop wood.
Be careful!
You're going to cut yourself!

75

Why do all within starve?
It is because ego taxes them for its own purpose.
Hence the hunger.

Why are all within hard to rule?
It is because ego makes demands upon them.
Hence the mutiny.

Why do all within seem suicidal?
It is because they are desperate to live.
Hence the recklessness.

One who values life for its own sake
is wiser than one who has other pursuits.

76

At birth a person is yin-yang;
at death, yang-yin.
All things in Nature are supple;
at death they are brittle.

Thus yang-yin belongs to the dead,
and yin-yang belongs to the living.
The rigid warriors are destroyed,
and the rigid trees snap.

Unyielding, "great" ego is lowlife.
The soft and yielding soar.

77

Yin-yang Way is like stretching a bow:
the upper part bends downward,
and the lower part is raised.
Excess and deficiency are adjusted,
and there is balance.

Yin-yang mind reduces ego-surplus,
and increases dream input.
To subsidize all within
is not the way of yang-yin.
Yang-yin takes from needy dreams
and donates to fat-cat ego.

Who can offer ego-riches to all within?
Only yin-yang mind.

Yin-yang mind does not grasp,
does not boast of what gets done.
Yin-yang mind is not a show-off.

78

Nothing is more yielding than water,
but for polishing driftwood
there's nothing like it.

Everybody knows
that "weak" is stronger than "strong."
Everybody knows
that Soft overcomes Hard.
People know this,
but ignore it.

Yin-yang mind sees lotus rooted in mud.
To undo the disasters of ego
you must lead Psyche beyond.

For yang-yin mind,
yin-yang truth is a paradox.

79

When yang-yin reconciles with yin-yang,
there will remain a scar.

Yin-yang mind asks,
"Is this good?"

Thus, yin-yang mind,
feeling like a debtor,
does not dun anyone.

Yin-yang mind has mana;
yang-yin mind has tax collectors.

Being impartial,
yin-yang mind favors all within.

80

Y in-yang mind is uncomplicated,
rather than complicated.
To all within,
the high-tech world serves no purpose.

All within love the home life,
and do not emigrate.
They have boats and cars,
but no travelers.
The War Machine is of no interest.
All within like the abacus.

Let them enjoy their food,
have their clothing,
like their dwellings,
and honor their customs.

Yin-yang and yang-yin are neighbors.
They hear each other's dogs and roosters,
and they keep their distance.

81

Tao truth is not sweet to big ego,
nor is flattery sweet to yin-yang ego.
What's to argue?

Yin-yang mind is not taught by others,
whereas yang-yin mind esteems the Ph.D.

Yin-yang mind holds nothing back:
the more it lives for all within,
the more abundant its life.

The Tao benefits,
it does not harm.
Yin-yang mind is not driven to win;
it just does its thing
by doing nothing.

COMMENTARIES

43

Yoni, the cushiest place of all,
subdues lingam,
the hardest throb of all.

The Cave pervades the spelunker.
Hence I know the value of Receptive Embrace.

Without words it teaches;
without ego-effort it fulfills.

Number 43 affords a good example of how the present version differs from the typical translations.

As Chen explains, Lao Tzu says literally, "The softest in the world,/ Gallops in the hardest in the world." The present version translates this erotically into yoni and lingam.

Horseback riding is a common metaphor for (1) inspiration (Pegasus), and (2) sexual activity. In both cases it means excited immersion in the river of libido.

The translators generally acknowledge that "soft" and "hard" refer universally to Water and Rock. Indeed, the River/Valley is Lao Tzu's favorite archetype. At the same time no man can fail to relate his own manhood to the idea of soft/hard. (Chinese erotica—"pillow books"—abounds with sexual metaphors taken from Nature.)

Besides Chen, two other translators retain the riding metaphor: Heysinger ("The softest thing . . . will gallop o'er"), and Mair ("The softest thing . . . gallops triumphantly over / The hardest thing").

Wu says, "The softest . . . overrides the hardest." Henricks says that

"The softest . . . runs roughshod over / the firmest." Five translators make this more abstract: the softest "overcomes" the hardest. Waley stresses the aggressive idea ("overwhelm"); Poynton stresses the more passive ("outlast").

Blakney says that the softest "penetrates" the hardest (despite the semantic resonance of penis/penetrate). Chu is the most abstract: "The nonexistent can enter into the impenetrable." Montagne, the most consistently extravert translator, says that "The most flexible elements of Society activate (*"hacen marchar"*) the most rigid elements of Society."

Well, then: does yin, as instinctual Self "activate" yang, the worldly ego? Does yin "enter into" yang? Penetrate it? "Outlast" it, "overwhelm" it, "overcome" it? Does yin "run roughshod" over yang—"override" it? Yin can do all these things in cases ranging from ecstasy to madness; Lao Tzu himself chooses to say that the softest gallops in the hardest, as Chen explains. If he is speaking at a universal level of meaning, then erotically yoni subdues lingam. "Lingam" means more than "penis"—it means "erection." When man and woman make love, the erection is subdued, and the man gratefully finds the great tension resolved.

The Cave and the Spelunker

What is a spelunker? "A person who explores caves, especially as a hobby." I like that dictionary afterthought—"especially as a hobby."

Spelunking is a "labor of love" (i.e., play). When the spelunker enters a cave, this is a form of enlightenment, or orgasm. "The Cave pervades the spelunker."

This is the whole idea—to enter the Cave and be pervaded by the loving embrace. This is a spiritual happiness bestowed by yin-yang mind: a sense of halcyon Oneness on a tranquil sea.

Paradox

However we translate the opening statement of 43, we are dealing with a paradox in any case, for Lao Tzu goes on to say, "That which is not penetrates that which has no crevice" (Chen).

This is a paradox, ¿no? The paradox is an "apparent contradiction." It is "apparent," because we realize that the statement is really a challenge to use our imagination and intelligence. If we hear that "only the poor are rich" we know that we are being challenged to rethink the meaning of "poor" and "rich."

So Lao Tzu writes, "That which is not /penetrates that which has no crevice." The translations all simply state the paradox in English ("The non-existent may enter the spaceless," and so forth). But a paradox begs to be resolved. In what sense are the poor rich? In what sense can non-being penetrate that which has no crevice?

Sexist male ego does not recognize Yin. Ego, full of itself, has no room left to accommodate Her. She should be an active participant in the life of ego, but masculine ego does not want to be sissified— watered down, as it were. Real men don't cry.

Whenever male ego is shocked into an awareness of Yin, it then suddenly realizes (along with Lao Tzu) that the "non-existent" has suddenly entered into a place where there was supposedly no opening:

> That which is not
> penetrates
> that which has no crevice.

This switch-over may occur as a shock, when male ego is suddenly traumatized, either by a negative event (tragedy) or a positive one (good pot). But no doubt most often the shock is a woman. She has Yin vibes, immediately recognized and valued. She, in effect, is his guru.

Usually yang-yin ego recovers its ascendancy, and that's the end of that. But in any case She truly pointed the Way, the Tao.

> That which seems to be non-existent
> may indeed penetrate
> that which seems to have no weak spots.

Running Commentary

1

When you speak of "your" psyche you put the cart before the horse. The Valley (Riverbed) is Lao Tzu's favorite archetype, the Land of Yoni. Mother Nature is the Valley. Her flowing created the Valley. Yin-yang mind gets into the Flow—skinny-dips. Yang-yin mind doesn't want to get its feet wet.

2

The "wise ones" are those who favor yin-yang mind where Nature (not ego) generates the climate. They do not try to possess Psyche; they embrace Her and feel Her embrace.

3

"Wisdom" means "ego-transcendent." Yin-yang ego and Mother Nature take dinner together.

4

Nature transcends the so-called "opposites." The lover is not "opposite" you; you and your lover are complements.

5

Yin-yang mind views ego as a dummy sitting on the knee of Cosmic Ventriloquist. Pope Mortimer.

6

Lao Tzu is on a trip, a voyage of discovery. He's saying, "Look, Ma! No hands!" He keeps getting new ideas about this revolution—the sudden switch from yang-yin to yin-yang. He can't believe his luck, as he says.

7

Each generation has its eccentricities. People want to be "up-to-date." Here I use flapper language and hippie language. They join in recommending that you transcend your time warp.

8

"Timing" means "natural rhythm." When a wave breaks on the shore, that is timing; so is coming in the arms of your lover.

9

Recognize what there is, not what you think there ought to be. This is very tricky, and can work like a koan. Think about the Goose that Laid the Golden Egg.

10

"Integrity," according to yang-yin ego, means "uncompromising adherence to moral principles" (dictionary).

"Integrity," according to yin-yang ego, means integrating ego with Psyche. Yang-yin ego is a Separatist.

11

The "space within" is the Creative Unconscious. As Juan Ramón Jiménez said, "Roots and wings, yes! / But the Roots should fly, / and the Wings should take root!"

12

Ego typically seeks gratification in terms of one of the five senses (voyeur, gourmet, masturbator, bulimic, and so forth). Beyond the five senses is Yin-yang Sense—the Common Sense—that underlies all the five senses.

13

Here Psyche speaks for Herself, in the First Person; likewise "all within." This is a recorded exchange between ego and Psyche. The very view expressed here underlies our nightly dream life.

14

Psyche speaks to ego, describing our dream life. When we dream we do all that She describes here. When we dream we live in the Now. This is life, like it or not.

15

Lao Tzu says, "In the old days." I understand this to mean, "In the days before ego took over."

16

This is an appeal to recognize Psyche as Mother Nature in human form.

17

Like the witch, the shaman lives deep within the instinctual Self. Urban ego (yang-yin mind) distrusts such people, and places all trust in its own leadership. The ancient Greeks called this hubris: ego-arrogance in the face of the gods.

18

Ignoring the ways of Nature, ego invents its own laws, loading the dice in its own favor. This is true especially of male ego, the source of patriarchy. The patriarchy invents its own God and claims to rule by divine right. "Patriotism" means more than love of *patria*; it means love of the Patriarch ("Thou shalt love thy God with all thy heart.")

19

The patriarch declares certain natural bents to be sinful, immoral, and illegal, just like any other tyrant with tunnel vision. Yin-yang ego says, "Relax."

20

It is a truism to say that yin-yang mind has no home in yang-yin world. Yin-yang mind is in the patriarchal world, but not of it, much like unwilling draftees in the army.

21

What Shelley said of poetry is true also of our dream life:

> Dreams compel us to feel
> that which we perceive,
> and to imagine
> that which we know.

When yang-yin ego declares dreams to be unreal, it is simply rejecting the instinctual Self.

22

"Have much, and lose the Way." This recalls the bumper sticker that says, "He who dies with the most toys wins." Yang-yin ego equates life with winning over other yang-yin egos. It calls this the "real world."

23

"Centripetal" = "seeking the Center." (L. *peto,* Eng. "petition," Sp. *pedir.*)
"Centri-fugal" = "fleeing the Center"(L. *fugio,* to flee).
Centripetal and centrifugal are two dynamic words that describe

the basic difference between yin-yang ego and yang-yin ego. Yang-yin ego is indeed a fugitive from Mother Nature—with no place on Earth to hide.

24

Yang-yin ego poisons the well of Psyche—hence it is "unwanted food." Psyche requires a yin-yang diet. To offer Her yang-yin is like offering steak to a vegetarian.

"We are not amused" is from Queen Victoria, of course. I attribute it to Queen Psyche as a kind of pleasant satire; Queen Victoria was such a patriarchal woman!

25

Yoni is the Great River/Valley, the Womb—as is the Creative Unconscious.

26

Yin-yang ego is the steward of Psyche, not Her master. The creative person functions in the yin-yang mode, being a midwife so to speak.

Gravity makes flight possible. The seagull does not "overcome" gravity, much less "conquer" it. She allows it to fulfill her.

27

In the nature of things yang-yin ego gives rise to yin-yang ego. This is the realization that deserting yang-yin ego really means transcending it. You are not being a traitor.

28

This piece was my first clue that the *Tao Te Ching* can be read as a feminist manifesto. Lao Tzu's advice seems to be clearly directed from one man to patriarchal readers.

The great tailor (artisan) begins with a fundamental respect for the material being used. You embody the qualities of the material, you take advantage of them. A great Pietà can show you marble weeping.

29

Yang-yin ego takes Earth for granted (just as Freud took dreaming for granted), so naturally Psyche becomes his property. After all, he invented the idea of real estate.

30

Yang-yin mind thinks in terms of power (might makes right). He is the general, and Psyche is his drafted army.

31

According to tradition Left Hand is *sinister,* as the Romans said. Yang-yin ego exists by reason of its mistrust of Instinct.

32

Know when enough is enough—meaning, know when enough ego is enough ego in the dynamics of Psyche.

33

The expression "your own ego" is semantically curious, ¿*no?* It is Psyche speaking to yang-yin ego.

34

It's an old Zen saying: "In Nature nobody does anything, yet everything gets done." It's the same thing with Psyche developing into an individual human being.

35

The popular American notion of tofu is correct symbol for Occidental idea of Asian viewpoint.

36

This piece refers to athletics. In martial arts you "grunt" as you exhale. Just like Monica Seles hitting the ball.

37

Wu-wei, "non-action," is basic to Taoist view (sometimes called "*wu-wei* philosophy"). I think that the term "ego-action" is useful for understanding the difference between yin-yang and yang-yin minds. "Inspirations" are *wu-wei*, not determined by ego-planning.

38

More on *wu-wei.* Yang-yin ego quickly becomes cut and dried, as when people in church nod off during the sermon. Tribal rituals actually evoke and reanimate the vital spirits. Yang-yin mind wants to forget Nature; yin-yang mind wants to rejoin Her.

39

This is written in the style of the charismatic preacher. Amen!

40

After 39, this is a gentle spiritual sung by the choir—the ones enslaved by Massa Ego. In yin-yang dance nobody "leads."

41

This piece contemplates the abyss separating yang-yin and yin-yang minds. Yin-yang mind is aware of the abyss; yang-yin mind is ignorant of any such thing. Yang-yin mind is lost in the illusion of its own self-worth.

42

Here Lao Tzu ends with a reference to the Sage, the Master, the Mentor. Such being the case, I wish to honor Lao Tzu. He says, "I honor the sage." I say, "Ditto, Lao Tzu."

43

This is Dance of Eros, a loving embrace. Yang-yin ego sees it as "performing." Yang-yin ego is always trying to prove something.

44

Yang-yin ego is not even aware that it is possible to evolve. When macho ego monopolizes the energy of Psyche, he is hoarding Her riches, refusing to let Her circulate freely as is Her Way.

45

Yin-yang mind exists in the living waters of Psyche; to yang-yin mind this appears to be a bent stick. Yang-yin mind is always looking for an angle.

46

"Enough is enough": a truism, ¿*no*? The truism uses semantic leverage to convince you of a special point of view: "Boys will be boys"; "When you're dead, you're dead"; "A promise is a promise"; "Enough is enough." Well, yin-yang ego knows when enough is enough.

47

"Achievement" means one thing to yang-yin ego, another to yin-yang mind.

48

"Empire" is a transcendentalist name for Centeredness or Integration. Sovereignty of Psyche is independent of patriarchal constraints.

49

Yin-yang mind does not practice repression in the name of self-image. "All within" are more important than "all out there."

50

Yang-yin ego lives by exploiting psychic energy. He is the Intruder, just as cancer is an intruder.

51

This is a Thanksgiving song by Lao Tzu and me.

52

In the Bible St. John says, "In the beginning was the Word. . . ." ("Word" is the translation of *logos*.) Transcendentalist experience knows better, as stated here.

53

Sometimes yang-yin ego's exploitation of Psyche's energy seems like a crime.

54

Individuating amounts to establishing a culture of one person. The existence of human culture does not depend upon numbers; one soul suffices.

55

"You make me feel like a virgin." That's yin-yang ego speaking.

56

This recalls formal meditation. "Simplify" is the key strategy. Yang-yin ego is complex; yin-yang ego is Simple (One).

57

Urban society is a projection of the mind of its rulers; yin-yang mind is laissez faire, since nobody "rules."

58

When ego governs too much, we get a Pentagon mentality. Patriarchs are hawks by nature, *¿no?*

59

This is a good example of Chinese Fortune-cookie style of writing the *Tao Te Ching*. There are no limits.

60

Male ego is like an angry teenage guy: he has to be defused.

61

Here "seduce" has the yin-yang meaning: "to raise consciousness."

62

Jehovah judges harshly; who needs it? Give me a break, old man!

63

From macho viewpoint Transcendentalism is a "slight to ego." Small wonder.

64

"Act now, having the luxury": this is *wu-wei*, non-action, i.e., non-ego action. This is play, which is the luxury of our life: indulgence in life itself, libido free of ego-goals.

65

As we experience the life of Psyche we need to be bilingual—able to speak both the language of yin-yang and of yang-yin; otherwise, Psyche's creative possibilities are closed to us.

66

Bad coach is concerned for his own standing (wins/losses). Good coach is concerned for the well-being of the team.

67

Yin-yang mind recognizes Motherly Love as the Earth Principle.

68

"Good" refers to non-ego action generated by the Creative Unconscious ("inspiration").

69

I spent time in the army (as a private) and it never occurred to me to underestimate the power of the Establishment—hell, I was in their toils! To this day I think of yang-yin ego as an officer, and of yin-yang ego as a draftee: I am *in* the army, but not *of* it!

70

For a lefty, writing with the left hand is easy, but very difficult for a right-handed person. This is a good metaphor for the idea behind 70.

71

Transcendental style favors paradox: "get sick of your sickness." *Para-dox* means "beyond common opinion." In the patriarchy yang-yin ego represents common opinion.

72

The difference between "self" and "Self" is a fact of life in the experience of yin-yang mind; yang-yin mind is unaware of any such distinction.

73

Yang-yin ego is the Evel Knievel of Psyche, the eternal teenage show-off. It thinks nothing of sacrificing Psyche on the altar of its own self-display.

74

Ego lives in clock time and dismisses phenomena outside its time frame (e.g., dreams). Within the Psyche "repression" = "punishment." Let Psyche do the repressing, as is Her Way; don't try to do it yourself.

75

Do not take life for granted, like men eating their steaks.

76

Yin-yang mind is always being born. Yang-yin mind is cut and dried.

77

In Psyche the "upper" (ego) bends downward, and the "lower" (Creative Unconscious) is raised—and there you have yin-yang mind, transcendentalist mind, shooting an arrow heavenward.

78

Ego-consciousness is a piece of driftwood borne on the ocean tides. The Individuation Process means being polished by the Great Waters, the Shining Big Sea Waters.

79

In Psyche is constant seesaw between ego-domination and freedom of Creative Unconscious. Like a seesaw this abrades the fulcrum. The scar is a sign of healing—but only yin-yang mind recognizes that any "healing" was necessary in the first place!

80

Psyche is inhabited by two people: yang-yin mind and yin-yang mind. No matter which one you may identify with—remain aware of your neighbor. This is the beginning of wisdom.

81

Lao Tzu's advice to ego: Laissez faire.

SOURCES

Bahm, Archie J. *Tao Teh King.* NY: F. Ungar, 1958

Blakney, R. B. *The Way of Life: Lao Tzu.* NY: New American Lib., 1955

Ch'u Ta-Kao. *Tao Te Ching: A New Translation.* London: G. Allen, 1937

Chen, Ellen M. *The Tao Te Ching: A New Translation with Commentary.* NY: Paragon House, 1989

Choy, Rita Mei-Wah. *Read and Write Chinese.* San Francisco: China West Books, 1990.

English, Jane, and Gia-Fu Feng. *Tao Te Ching.* NY: Vintage Books, 1972

Henricks, Robert G. *Lao-Tzu. Te-Tao Ching: A New Translation.* NY: Ballantine Books, 1989

Heysinger, I. W. *The Light of China: The Tao Teh King of Lao Tsze.* Philadelphia: Research Pub. Co., 1903

Legge, James. *The Texts of Taoism.* NY: The Julian Press, 1959

Mair, Victor H. *Tao Te Ching: The Classic Book of Integrity and the Way.* NY: Bantam Books, 1990

Medhurst, C. Spurgeon. *The Tao-Teh-King: Sayings of Lao-Tzu.* London: The Theosophical Pub. House, 1905

Mitchell, Stephen. *Tao Te Ching.* NY: Harper, 1988

Montagne, Edmundo. *El libro del sendero y de la línea-recta.* Buenos Aires: Editorial Kier, 1947

Poynton, Orde. *The Great Sinderesis, being a translation of Tao Te Ching.* Adelaide: Hassell Press, 1949.

Waley, Arthur. *The Way and Its Power: a study of Tao Te Ching.* NY: Grove Press, 1958.

Wu, John C. W. *Lao Tzu/Tao Te Ching.* NY: St John's Univ. Press, 1961